My nine Book

THE CHILD'S WORLD

ELGIN, ILLINOIS 60120

by Jane Belk Moncure
illustrated by Linda Hohag
and Dan Spoden

Editor: Diane Dow Suire

Distributed by Childrens Press, 1224 West Van Buren Street, Chicago, Illinois 60607.

Library of Congress Cataloging in Publication Data

Moncure, Jane Belk.
  My nine book.

  (My number books / Jane Belk Moncure)
  Summary: Little Nine introduces the concept of
"nine" by interacting with nine of a variety of things
which group and regroup to demonstrate principles of
adding and subtracting.
    1. Nine (The number)—Juvenile literature.
[1. Nine (The number)   2. Number concept.   3. Counting]
I. Hohag, Linda, ill.   II. Title.   III. Title: My 9 book.
IV. Series: Moncure, Jane Belk.   My number books.
QA141.3.M674 1986   513'.2 [E]   85-30959
ISBN 0-89565-320-6

2 3 4 5 6 7 8 9 10 11 12 R 91 90 89 88 87

My  Book

This is Little nine.

He lives in the house of nine.

The house of nine has nine rooms.

Count them.

Every day Little  goes for a walk. One day he walks to the park. He sees

two toy astronauts on a bench . . .

and seven toy astronauts
sitting under a tree.
How many all together?

The next day Little  sees them again.
Now they are sad.

"We have lost our spaceships!" they say.
"We need them for the toy parade."

"I will help you," says Little .
He hops five hops on one
foot and four hops on the other foot.
Can you?

Guess where he finds the first toy spaceship?

He finds the second, third, fourth and fifth spaceships . . .

under a bridge.

Now five toy astronauts
hop into their toy spaceships.

"Wait," says Little  .

"Wait for the other astronauts!" How many?

Little  finds the sixth, seventh, eighth and ninth toy spaceships in a sandbox in the park.

The four toy astronauts are happy.

Then away fly all the toy astronauts in their
spaceships. Count them.

"Watch the parade!" they shout.

Little  hops six hops on one foot . . .
and three hops on the other foot.
Can you?

Guess what he finds.

He finds toy soldiers standing in a line.
They are very sad.

"The toy parade is about to begin . . .
and we have lost our nine drums," they say.

"I will help you," says Little  .

He finds six drums . . .

under a picnic table. How many are still lost?

Now six happy soldiers beat their drums.
"Tum-tum-tum, tum-tum-tum."

"Wait!" says Little nine.

"Wait for the other drummers."
How many more?

Little  finds . . .

two drums under the leaves . . .

and one  behind a rock.

Now will each soldier have a drum?

As the happy soldiers march away, they say,
"Come to the toy parade today!"

Count the soldiers.

Little 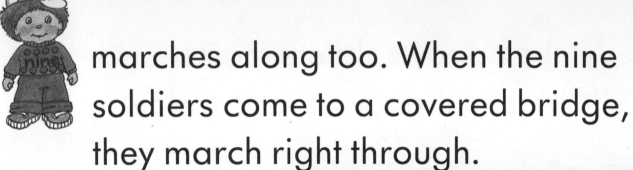 marches along too. When the nine soldiers come to a covered bridge, they march right through.

How many are inside the
covered bridge?

How many are on the outside?

Then they march right down the street. The toy parade begins at last.

Little nine waves as the soldiers march past.

The toy astronauts fly by and drop balloons from the sky. How many?

Little  runs after the balloons.

He catches five.

"I want to catch all of them," he says.

He catches
four
more.

Does he have
nine?

"I can be an astronaut and fly," he says.
He holds the balloons very high.

He runs to the top of a hill.
"I want to fly," he says.
He jumps nine high jumps.
Can you?

He does not fly. "Pop, pop, pop, pop, pop," go some balloons. How many?

How many balloons are left?

Guess what? A real astronaut comes by.
"I will help you," she says.

"I will take you for a ride in a real
spaceship. Step inside."

"Count down! Nine, eight, seven, six, five, four, three, two, one. Blast off!"

Away they go Zoom!

Let's add with Little  .

$$\begin{array}{r} 2 \\ + 7 \\ \hline 9 \end{array}$$

$$\begin{array}{r} 1 \\ + 8 \\ \hline 9 \end{array}$$

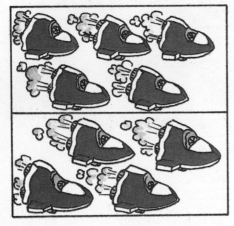

$$\begin{array}{r} 5 \\ + 4 \\ \hline 9 \end{array}$$

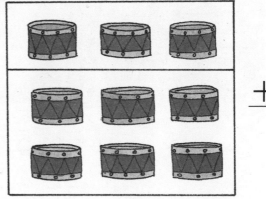

$$\begin{array}{r} 3 \\ + 6 \\ \hline 9 \end{array}$$

Now you add nine things together in other ways.

Extra Pages

Let's take away with Little .

$$\begin{array}{r} 9 \\ -\ 4 \\ \hline 5 \end{array}$$

$$\begin{array}{r} 9 \\ -\ 3 \\ \hline 6 \end{array}$$

$$\begin{array}{r} 9 \\ -\ 5 \\ \hline 4 \end{array}$$

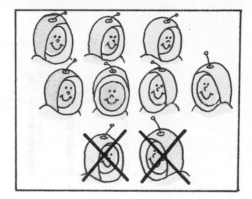

$$\begin{array}{r} 9 \\ -\ 2 \\ \hline 7 \end{array}$$

Now you find other ways to take away from nine.

Little  can make a 9. Here's how:

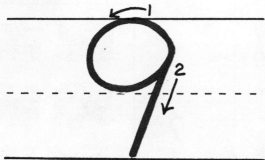

He can make the number word nine. Here's how:

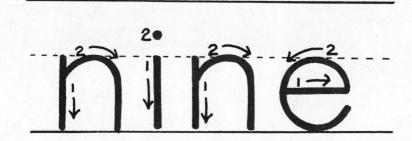

You can make them in the air with your finger.